I0790892

Speech Freedom

Abuse of the First Amendment: Speech Freedom

Jess Browning

Bainbridge Island, WA 98110

Speech Freedom

Bronco ePublishing, LLC
Bainbridge Island, Washington

Abuse of the First Amendment: Speech Freedom

ISBN-13: 978-1981637478
ISBN-10: 1981637478

First published 2017.

www.broncoepublishing.com.

Some copyright material referenced is under terms of the GNU Free Documentation License http://en.wikipedia.org/wiki/GNU_Free_Documentation_License.

For Creative Commons Licenses see their websites http://creativecommons.org/licenses/by-sa/2.0/deed.en and http://creativecommons.org/licenses/by-sa/3.0/

Terror, extreme, sharia, decisions, war, police

Abuse of the First Amendment

Speech Freedom

BOOKS IN PRINT

Black & White Non-fiction

Technology, the Economy & Jobs: A Historical Perspective
Ancient European Ancestors (A Grey Tones Edition)
Brownings in England (A Grey Tones Edition)
Captain John Browning (A Grey Tones Edition)
Jess and his Family: Genealogy and History (Grey Tones Edition)
Global Logistics and Trade: Intermodal Transport
The Innovation Process: Educating and Teaching
Respect for Labor
The Deceitful and Insidious Web
Seattle to England by Surface Transport
King Arthur & Modred: A Young King in Waiting
King Arthur & Sir Balin: A Knight with Two Swords
King Arthur & Pellianore: A Father of Knights
King Arthur & Sir Gawaine: Their Adventures
King Arthur & Rome: Ambassadors Demand Tribute
King Arthur & Lancelot: Their Fights & Affairs
King Arthur & **Gareth***: The Kitchen Boy*
King Arthur & Tristram: The Fighter
King Arthur & Knights: Lovers and Fighters

Color Non-fiction

Ancient European Ancestors: The DNA, Archeological, Historical and Linguistic Evidence

Browning's in England: Records of where, when & how they lived

Captain John Browning: A Family History in England & Virginia from 1255 to 1799 AD

Jess and his Family: Genealogy and History

Black & White Historical Fiction: Short Stories

The Nomads: Their Migration Experiences

The Anglos: Their Pleasures and Travails

Southwest England: Life and Times 1390 to 1430 AD

Captain John: From England to Virginia

Francis: Plantation Owner, Merchant & Tobacco Farmer

Caleb: The Frontier Man

Jeb: His Family and History

William T.: A Man to Look up to

China: 1979

Black & White Collected Short Stories

Anatolia to Britain: A Trilogy

America's Frontier: Virginia to California

Compendium of Short Stories: From Eurasia to Seattle

Black & White Biographies

Life and Times of Jess Sr.

Life and Times of Anna Love.

Jess Jr.: A DIY Guy

Cec and Caroline: A Wonderful Life!

Vicki: A Cheerleader

Some Swank Descendants

Some Perdue Descendants

Books Edited & Re-written

Four Centuries 1611-2017: The English Bible

King Arthur Series Volume One

King Arthur & Modred: A Young King in Waiting
King Arthur & Sir Balin: A Knight with Two Swords
King Arthur & Pellianore: A Father of Knights
King Arthur & Sir Gawain: Their Adventures
King Arthur & Rome: Ambassadors Demand Tribute
King Arthur & Lancelot: Their Fights & Affairs
King Arthur & **Gareth***: The Kitchen Boy*
King Arthur & Tristram: The Fighter
King Arthur & Knights: Lovers & Fighters

King Arthur Series Volume Two

King Arthur & Lancelot: Book X, Volume Two
King Arthur & Lancelot: Book XI, Volume Two
King Arthur & Lancelot: Book XII, Volume Two
King Arthur & Lancelot: Book XIII, Volume Two
King Arthur: Percivale: & Lancelot Books XIV-XV, Vol. Two
King Arthur & Gawain: Book XVI, Volume Two
King Arthur & Galahad: Book XVII, Volume Two
King Arthur & Queen's Joy: Book XVIII, Volume Two
King Arthur: Guinevere & Lancelot Book XIX, Volume Two
King Arthur & Gawain: Book XX, Volume Two
King Arthur & Mordred: Book XXI, Volume Two

Speech Freedom

CONTENTS

Abuse of the First Amendment

Speech Freedom

DEDICATION

This book is dedicated to all who have endured the time spent by the author on its research, writing, editing and publication.

It is especially dedicated to my wife Vicki, my daughters Carrie, Alexa, Nanci and Susan as well as to grandchildren, sisters, relatives, ancestors and friends.

The book is also dedicated to the referenced sources noted which were of great help in providing a work that is hoped to be of educational value to the broader community. The inclusion of these sources adds immensely to the story presented in a critical manner and the brief nature of its inclusion has no reflection on its value.

Specific citations are given when information is available and when not available credit is given based on the source.

Speech Freedom

INTRODUCTION

The First Amendment to the United States Constitution prevents Congress from making any law respecting an establishment of religion, prohibiting the free exercise of religion, or abridging the freedom of speech, the freedom of the press, the right to peaceably assemble, or to petition for a governmental redress of grievances. It was adopted on December 15, 1791, as one of the ten amendments that constitute the Bill of Rights.

This book focuses on Freedom of Speech.

Speech Freedom

CHAPTER ONE: Changes[1]

The definition of *freedom* in America has been evolving since the birth of the nation, historian Eric Foner said at the sixth annual Law and Humanities Distinguished Lecture, presented by the USC Center for Law, History and Culture.

Foner is one of the most prominent historians in the United States. He received his doctorate from Columbia in 1969. He is one of only two persons to serve as president of the three major professional organizations: the American Historical Association, Organization of American Historians, and Society of American Historians.

Lori Craig, a reporter for USC News, stated that Foner presented a number of meanings and interpretations given to the core American value in his speech. He said that the idea of freedom in American History, 1776-2007 is a tale of debates and disagreements and conflicts and controversies. That the meaning of freedom has been fought out, battled over, at every level of society — from Supreme Court decisions and Congressional debates down to labor picket lines, and even in bedrooms.

Foner pointed to several events in American history when the definition of freedom underwent a change. The revolution revealed an inner contradiction of American freedom by giving birth to a republic founded on liberty but economically was resting in large measure on slavery.

Freedom came to be defined more and more by the boundary of race and slavery which shaped the language and idea of freedom. He said that terms like *wage slavery* and *sex slavery* exist because *slavery* came to embody the notion of a lack of freedom.

The modern idea of freedom was created by the abolitionists and at the end of slavery discussions of freedom turned to economic autonomy and the free market.

The free person is one who is able to compete without any restriction in the economic marketplace for personal advancement. Foner said that President Franklin D. Roosevelt, linked liberty to economic security and equality.

About World War II the Bill of Rights seemed to be re-discovered that reinvigorated the idea of freedom as protecting civil liberties, such as the right of dissent and freedom of speech. The fight against the Nazis and their theory of a master race once again put the question of racial justice on the national agenda and freedom in America was said to rest on tolerance and equality.

When the Cold War and the USSR replaced Germany as the enemy of freedom and the socialist idea of *freedom from want* became suspect, the economic definition of freedom shifted back to *free enterprise.* Foner pointed to the famous 1959 kitchen debate between Nixon and Khrushchev as the point of the consumer's definition of freedom.

The civil rights movement also rediscovered freedom as a rallying cry for the dispossessed which elevated the idea of personal, private freedom into a political freedom.

Most recently, the terrorist attacks of 9/11 spurred another turn in the history of freedom.

Foner said that the language of freedom again took center stage in our public discourse. That freedom became the sort of all-purpose explanation for both the attack of Sept. 11 and the ensuing war against terror. There was a notion that the terrosist is against our freedom, he is an enemy of freedom that is very powerful and old in American history.

Abuse of the First Amendment

Speech Freedom

CHAPTER TWO: Article, The[2]

As mentioned in the introduction, the First Amendment bars Congress from preventing the freedom of speech, or of the press. A U.S. Supreme Court Justice commented about this phraseology in a 1993 journal article that said the word *'the'* in the term *'the freedom of speech'* suggests that the draftsmen intended to protect an identified category or subset of speech because of the definitive article. Otherwise, the clause could protect things like false testimony under oath.

A journalist said that the word *the* can be read to mean what was understood at the time to be included in the concept of free speech. But what was understood at the time is not exactly clear. In the late 1790s, the lead author of speech and press clauses, James Madison, argued against narrowing this freedom to what had existed under English common law:

The practice in America must be entitled to much more respect. In every state, probably, in the Union, the press has exerted a freedom in canvassing the merits and measures of public men, of every description, which has not been confined to the strict limits of the common law.

Madison wrote this in 1799, when he was in a dispute about the constitutionality of the *Alien and Sedition Laws*, which was legislation enacted in 1798 by President John Adams' Federalist Party to ban seditious libel. Madison believed that legislation to be unconstitutional, and his adversaries in that dispute, such as John Marshall, advocated the narrow freedom of speech that had existed in the English common law.

Abuse of the First Amendment

CHAPTER THREE: Gov't Criticism[3]

The Supreme Court refused to rule on the constitutionality of any federal law regarding the Free Speech Clause until the 20th century. For example, the Supreme Court never ruled on the Alien and Sedition Acts. Sedition is the conduct or speech inciting people to rebel against the authority of a state or monarch. The Alien and Sedition Acts were four bills passed by the Federalist-dominated 5th United States Congress and signed into law by President John Adams in 1798. They made it harder for an immigrant to become a citizen, allowed the president to imprison and deport non-citizens who were deemed dangerous or who were from a hostile nation. It included those making false statements that were critical of the federal government as outlined in the Sedition Act of 1798. Three Supreme Court justices riding circuit presided over the trials without indicating any reservations. The leading critics of the law, Vice President Thomas Jefferson and James Madison, argued for the Acts' unconstitutionality based on the First

Amendment and other Constitutional provisions.

Jefferson succeeded Adams as president, in part due to the unpopularity of the latter's sedition prosecutions; he and his party quickly overturned the Acts and pardoned those imprisoned by them. In a majority opinion in 1964, the Court noted the importance of the earlier public debate as a precedent in First Amendment law. Although the Sedition Act was never tested in the Supreme Court, the attack on the validity of the Act has precluded prosecution in the court.

In War

During the patriotic fervor of World War I and the First Red Scare, the Espionage Act of 1917 imposed a maximum sentence of twenty years on anyone who caused or attempted to cause insubordination, disloyalty, mutiny, or refusal of duty in the military or naval forces of the United States. Specifically, the Espionage Act of 1917 states that if anyone allows enemies to enter or fly over the United States and obtain information from a place connected with the national defense, they would be punished. Hundreds of prosecutions followed. In 1919, the Supreme Court heard four appeals resulting from cases that were prosecuted.

In the first of these cases, a Socialist Party of America official had been convicted under the Espionage Act for publishing leaflets urging resistance to the draft. The case was appealed, arguing that the Espionage Act violated the Free Speech Clause of the First Amendment. The Supreme Court unanimously rejected the appeal and affirmed the conviction. This conviction continued to be debated over whether the offical went against the right to freedom of speech protected by the First Amendment. The Chief Justice writing for the Court, explained that the question in every case of this type is whether the words used are of such a nature as to create a clear and present danger that they will bring about the substantive evils that Congress has a right to prevent. One week later, the court again upheld an Espionage Act conviction, this time regarding a journalist who had criticized U.S. involvement in foreign wars.

The Court elaborated on the *clear and present danger* test established in in the earlier offical's case. In 1918, a political activist, delivered a speech in Canton, Ohio, in which he spoke of loyal comrades who were paying the penalty of the working class, three individuals, who had been convicted of aiding and abetting in failing to register for the draft. Following a speech by one of the defendants, the person was charged and convicted under the Espionage Act. In upholding his conviction, the Court reasoned that although he had not spoken any words that posed a *clear and present danger*, taken in context, the speech had a *natural tendency and a probable effect to obstruct the recruiting services*. In another case, four Russian refugees appealed their conviction for throwing leaflets from a building in New York; the leaflets that argued against President Woodrow Wilson's intervention in Russia against the October Revolution. The majority upheld their conviction, but two justices dissented, holding that the government had demonstrated no *clear and present danger* in the four's political advocacy. Regarding Wilson: In 1917, the United States entered the war on the Allied side and President Woodrow Wilson dropped his reservations about joining the war and the United States began providing economic and technical support to the Provisional Russian Government. The Provisional Government ceased to exist when the Bolsheviks gained power following the October Revolution.

Passing Protection Along

The Supreme Court denied a number of *Free Speech Clause* claims throughout the 1920s, including the appeal of a labor organizer who had been convicted after distributing a manifesto calling for a *revolutionary dictatorship of the proletariat.* The Court upheld the conviction, but a majority also found that the First Amendment applied to state laws as well as federal laws, via the *Due Process Clause of the Fourteenth Amendment.* Two justices dissented in several more cases in this decade, however, advancing the argument that the Free Speech Clause protected a far greater range of political speech than the Court had previously acknowledged. In a 1927 case, a Communist Party USA organizer had been arrested for *criminal syndicalism*, this was followed by a justice who wrote a dissent in which it argued for broader protections for political speech.

The speech read: *Those who won our independence . . . believed that freedom to think as you will and to speak as you think are means indispensable to the discovery and spread of political truth; that without free speech and assembly discussion would be futile; that with them, discussion affords ordinarily adequate protection against the dissemination of noxious doctrine; that the greatest menace to freedom is an inert people; that public discussion is a political duty; and that this should be a fundamental principle of the American government.*

In 1937, the Court heard the case of an African American Communist Party organizer who had been convicted under the Slave Insurrection Statute for advocating black rule in the southern United States. In a 5–4 decision, the Court reversed the conviction, holding that Georgia had failed to demonstrate that there was any *clear and present danger* in the organizer's political advocacy.

In 1940, Congress enacted the Smith Act, making it illegal to advocate *the propriety of overthrowing or destroying any government in the United States by force and violence.* The statute provided a law enforcement tool to combat Communist leaders. After an organizer was convicted for attempting to organize a Communist Party, he petitioned for a writ, where the Court reviews a decision of a lower court, which the Supreme Court granted. In future cases the Court stated *In each case courts must ask whether the gravity of the 'evil', discounted by its improbability, justifies such invasion of free speech as necessary to avoid the danger.* One justice suggested that clear and present danger did not intimate *that before the Government may act, it must wait until the violent overthrow or putsch is about to be executed, the plans have been laid and the signal is awaited.* In a concurring opinion, another justice proposed a *balancing test*, which soon supplanted the *clear and present danger* test:

The demands of free speech in a democratic society as well as the interest in national security are better served by candid and informed weighing of the competing interests, within the confines of the judicial process.

The Alien Registration Act, popularly known as the *Smith Act*, was a United States federal statute that was enacted on June 29, 1940. It set criminal penalties for advocating the overthrow of the U.S. government and required all non-citizen adult residents to register with the government. The law was repealed in 1952. The Supreme Court limited the Smith Act prosecutions to *advocacy of action* rather than *advocacy in the realm of ideas*. Advocacy of abstract doctrine remained protected while speech explicitly inciting the forcible overthrow of the government was punishable under the Smith Act.

During the Vietnam War, the Court's position on public criticism of the government changed drastically. Though the Court upheld a law prohibiting the forgery, mutilation, or destruction of draft cards in United States fearing that burning of draft cards would interfere with the *smooth and efficient functioning* of the draft system, the next year, in 1969, the court handed down its decision in expressly overruling a 1968 decision. Now the Supreme Court referred to the right to speak openly of violent action and revolution in broad terms:

The decision reads: *Our decisions have fashioned the principle that the constitutional guarantees of free speech and free press do not allow a State to forbid or proscribe advocacy of the use of force or law violation except where such advocacy is directed to inciting or producing imminent lawless action and is likely to incite or cause such action.*

Brandenburg discarded the *clear and present danger* test introduced earlier. In 1971, the Court voted 5–4 to reverse the conviction of a man wearing a jacket reading *Fuck the Draft* in the corridors of a Los Angeles County courthouse. One justice wrote in the majority opinion that the man's jacket fell in the category of protected political speech despite the use of an expletive saying *one man's vulgarity is another man's lyric.*

Speech Freedom

CHAPTER FOUR: Politicians[4]

Literature

In 1960, the Court struck down a Los Angeles city ordinance that made it a crime to distribute anonymous pamphlets. One justice wrote in the majority opinion: *There can be no doubt that such an identification requirement would tend to restrict freedom to distribute information and thereby freedom of expression . . . . Anonymous pamphlets, leaflets, brochures and even books have played an important role in the progress of mankind.*

In 1995, the Court struck down an Ohio statute that made it a crime to distribute anonymous campaign literature. However, in an earlier decision (1987), the Court upheld the Foreign Agents Registration Act of 1938, under which several Canadian films were defined as *political propaganda,* requiring their sponsors to be identified.

Finance

In 1976, the Supreme Court reviewed the Federal Election Campaign Act of 1971 and related laws, which restricted the monetary contributions that may be made to political campaigns and expenditure by candidates. The Court affirmed the constitutionality of limits on campaign contributions, stating that they *served the basic governmental interest in safeguarding the integrity of the electoral process without directly impinging upon the rights of individual citizens and candidates to engage in political debate and discussion.* However, the Court overturned the spending limits, which it found imposed *substantial restraints on the quantity of political speech.*

The court again scrutinized campaign finance regulation in 2003. The case centered on the Bipartisan Campaign Reform Act of 2002 (BCRA), a federal law that imposed new restrictions on campaign financing. The Supreme Court upheld provisions which barred the raising of soft money by national parties and the use of soft money by private organizations to fund certain advertisements related to elections. However, the Court struck down the *choice of expenditure* rule, which required that parties could either make coordinated expenditures for all its candidates, or permit candidates to spend independently, but not both, which the Court agreed *placed an unconstitutional burden on the parties' right to make unlimited independent expenditures*. The Court also ruled that the provision preventing minors from making political contributions was unconstitutional.

In 2007, the Court sustained an *as applied* challenge to BCRA, holding that issue ads may not be banned from the months preceding a primary or general election. In 2008, the Supreme Court declared the *Millionaire's Amendment* provisions of the BCRA to be unconstitutional. The Court held that easing BCRA restrictions for an opponent of a self-financing candidate spending at least $350,000 of his or her own money violated the freedom of speech of the self-financing candidate.

The Bipartisan Campaign Reform Act (BCRA) is a federal law that amended the Federal Election Campaign Act, which regulates the financing of political campaigns. Its chief sponsors were two senators Senators. The law became effective in 2002 and the new legal limits became effective in 2003. In 2010, the Court ruled that the BCRA's federal restrictions on electoral advocacy by corporations or unions were unconstitutional for violating the Free Speech Clause of the First Amendment.

In 2014, the Court ruled that federal aggregate limits on how much a person can donate to candidates, political parties, and political action committees, combined respectively in a two-year period known as an *election cycle*, violated the Free Speech Clause of the First Amendment.

Flag desecration

The divisive issue of flag desecration as a form of protest first came before the Supreme Court in 1969. In response to hearing an erroneous report of the murder of a civil rights activist, a person burned a 48-star U.S. flag. The person was arrested and charged with a New York state law making it a crime *publicly to mutilate, deface, defile, or defy, trample upon, or cast contempt upon either by words or act any flag of the United States.* In a 5–4 decision, the Court, relying on a 1931 decision, found that because the provision of the New York law criminalizing *words* against the flag was unconstitutional, and the trial did not sufficiently demonstrate that the person was convicted solely under the provisions not yet deemed unconstitutional, the conviction was unconstitutional. The Court, however, *resisted the efforts to decide the constitutional issues involved in this case on a broader basis* and left the constitutionality of flag-burning unaddressed.

The ambiguity with regard to flag-burning statutes was eliminated in a 1989 case. In that case, a person burned an American flag at a demonstration during the 1984 Republican National Convention in Dallas, Texas. The person was charged with violating a Texas law prohibiting the vandalizing of venerated objects and was convicted, sentenced to one year in prison, and fined $2,000. The Supreme Court reversed his conviction in a 5–4 vote. One justice wrote in the decision that: *if there is a bedrock principle underlying the First Amendment, it is that government may not prohibit the expression of an idea simply because society finds the idea offensive or disagreeable.* Congress then passed a federal law barring flag burning, but the Supreme Court struck it down as well in 1990. A Flag Desecration Amendment to the U.S. Constitution has been proposed repeatedly in Congress since 1989, and in 2006 failed to pass the Senate by a single vote.

Falsifying military awards

While the unauthorized wear or sale of the Medal of Honor has been a punishable offense under federal law since the early 20th century, the Stolen Valor Act criminalized the act of not only wearing, but also verbally claiming entitlement to military awards that a person did not in fact earn. In 2012, the Supreme Court struck down the Act, ruling that the First Amendment bars the government from punishing people for making false claims regarding military service or honors where the false claim was not *made to effect a fraud or secure moneys or other valuable considerations.* The decision was a 6–3 ruling, but the six justices in the majority could not agree on a single rationale for it.

CHAPTER FIVE: Forcing[5]

The Supreme Court has determined that the First Amendment also protects citizens from being compelled to say or pay for certain speech. For example, in 1943, the Supreme Court ruled that school children could not be punished for refusing either to say the pledge of allegiance or salute the American flag. Compelled speech is a legal term.

The Pledge of Allegiance is an oath of allegiance to the United States that is addressed to both the flag and the Republic. It was composed by Rear Admiral George Balch in 1887, and was revised by Francis Bellamy in 1892. In 1942 it was formally adopted by Congress. Congress gave it the name *The Pledge of Allegiance* in 1945. In 1954 the words *under God* were added. Though many countries have oaths of allegiances for specific purposes, the US remains one of the few to use such an oath in childhood education.

Speech Freedom

CHAPTER SIX: Money in Talking[6]

Commercial speech is speech done on behalf of a company or individual for the purpose of making a profit. Unlike political speech, the Supreme Court does not afford commercial speech full protection under the First Amendment. To effectively distinguish commercial speech from other types of speech for purposes of litigation, the Court uses a list of four indicia (Signs, indications or circumstances which point to the existence of a given fact as probable, but not certain. For example, *indicia of partnership* are any circumstances which would induce the belief that a given person was in reality, though not ostensibly, a member of a given firm).

They include:

The contents do *no more than propose a commercial transaction.*

The contents may be characterized as advertisements.

The contents reference a specific product.

The disseminator is economically motivated to distribute the speech.

Alone, each indicium does not compel the conclusion that an instance of speech is commercial; however, *the combination of all these characteristics provides strong support for the conclusion that the speech is properly characterized as commercial speech.*

In 1942, the Court upheld a New York City ordinance forbidding the *distribution in the streets of commercial and business advertising matter.*

Writing for a unanimous court, a justice explained:

This court has unequivocally held that streets are proper places for the exercise of the freedom of communicating information and disseminating opinion and that, though the states and municipalities may appropriately regulate the privilege in the public interest, they may not unduly burden or proscribe its employment in their public thoroughfares. We are equally clear that the Constitution imposes no such restraint on government as respects purely commercial advertising.

In 1976, the Court ruled that commercial speech was entitled to First Amendment protection:

What is at issue is whether a State may completely suppress the dissemination of concededly truthful information about entirely lawful activity, fearful of that information's effect upon its disseminators and its recipients.

In 1978, the Court ruled that commercial speech was not protected by the First Amendment as much as other types of speech:

We have not discarded the common-sense distinction between speech proposing a commercial transaction, which occurs in an area traditionally subject to government regulation, and other varieties of speech. To require a parity of constitutional protection for commercial and noncommercial speech alike could invite a dilution, simply by a leveling process, of the force of the First Amendment's guarantee with respect to the latter kind of speech.

In 1980, the Court clarified what analysis was required before the government could justify regulating commercial speech:

Is the expression protected by the First Amendment? Lawful? Misleading? Fraud?

Is the asserted government interest substantial?

Does the regulation directly advance the governmental interest asserted?

Is the regulation more extensive than is necessary to serve that interest?

Six years later, the Court affirmed the Supreme Court of Puerto Rico's conclusion that Puerto Rico's Games of Chance Act of 1948, including the regulations thereunder, was not unconstitutional. The lax interpretation of the ruling was soon restricted in 1996, when the Court invalidated a Rhode Island law prohibiting the publication of liquor prices.

Speech Freedom

CHAPTER SEVEN: Education[7]

In 1969, the Supreme Court extended free speech rights to students in school. The case involved several students who were punished for wearing black armbands to protest the Vietnam War. The Court ruled that the school could not restrict symbolic speech that did not *materially and substantially* interrupt school activities. One justice wrote:

First Amendment rights, applied in light of the special characteristics of the school environment, are available to teachers and students. It can hardly be argued that either students or teachers shed their constitutional rights to freedom of speech or expression at the schoolhouse gate . . . . Schools may not be enclaves of totalitarianism. School officials do not possess absolute authority over their students. Students . . . are possessed of fundamental rights which the State must respect, just as they themselves must respect their obligations to the State.

In 1972, the Court ruled that Central Connecticut State College's refusal to recognize a campus chapter of Students for a

Democratic Society was unconstitutional, reaffirming the earlier decision.

However, since 1969 the Court has also placed several limitations on that ruling. In 1986, the Court ruled that a student could be punished for his sexual-innuendo-laced speech before a school assembly and, in 1988, the Court found that schools need not tolerate student speech that is inconsistent with their basic educational mission. In 2007, the Court ruled that schools could, consistent with the First Amendment, restrict student speech at school-sponsored events, even events away from school grounds, if students promote *illegal drug use.*

Speech Freedom

CHAPTER EIGHT: The Web[8]

In 2017, the Supreme Court held that a North Carolina law prohibiting registered sex offenders from accessing various websites impermissibly restricted lawful speech in violation of the First Amendment. The Court held that *a fundamental principle of the First Amendment is that all persons have access to places where they can speak and listen, and then, after reflection, speak and listen once more.*

The author would like to point out however, that the internet is a descietful and insidious place to visit. It is not for everyone, especially children, whose parents have limited ability to protect their children from visiting such places.

First of all, let me say that not all of the *web or internet* is deceitful or insidious – only portions of it are that way. It is used successfully by hundreds of millions of people worldwide for communicating by email, for *surfing or browsing,* for online purchasing, and for keeping in touch with others through social media sites like, Facebook, LinkedIn, Twitter, Google, etc. or just *surfing* the web for information.

The web is short for the *world wide web* (www) that is an information source where documents and other resources are often linked by hypertext and are accessed via the internet. Common sites are *web browsers* and home pages.

The problem is that the new industry spawned by the internet is seemingly more interested in making money than offering a service. What used to be free web access will probably become fee based. Of course most internet users today are paying a fee to be connected to the internet and email through a hosted server.[9]

Speech Freedom

CHAPTER NINE: Naughty Stuff[10]

One Supreme Court Justice wrote that while he could not precisely define pornography, he *knew it when he saw it.*

The federal government and the states have long been permitted to limit obscenity or pornography. While the Supreme Court has generally refused to give obscenity any protection under the First Amendment, pornography is subject to little regulation. However, the definitions of obscenity and pornography have changed over time.

In 1896, the Supreme Court adopted the same obscenity standard as had been articulated in a famous British case, in 1868. In that case a test defined material as obscene if it tended *to deprave or corrupt those whose minds are open to such immoral influences, and into whose hands a publication of this sort may fall.* In the early twentieth century, literary works were banned for obscenity. In a federal district court case in 1933, a new standard was established to evaluate a novel dated 1922, stating that works must be considered in their entirety, rather than declared obscene on the basis of an individual part of the work.

The Supreme Court ruled in 1957 that the First Amendment did not protect obscenity. It also ruled that the Brtish test was inappropriate; instead, a new test for obscenity was *whether to the average person, applying contemporary community standards, the dominant theme of the material, taken as a whole, appeals to the prurient interest.* This definition proved hard to apply, however, and in the following decade, members of the Court often reviewed films individually in a court building screening room to determine if they should be considered obscene.

The new test was expanded when the Court made a decision in 1973. Under the revised test, a work is obscene if:

(a) . . . 'the average person, applying contemporary community standards' would find the work, as a whole, appeals to the prurient interest . . . (b) . . . the work depicts or describes, in a patently offensive way, sexual

conduct specifically defined by the applicable state law, and (c) . . . the work, taken as a whole, lacks serious literary, artistic, political, or scientific value.

Note that *community* standards, not national standards, are applied whether the material appeals to the prurient interest, leaving the question of obscenity to local authorities. Child pornography is not subject to the Miller test, as the Supreme Court decided in 1982 and 1990 ruling that the government's interest in protecting children from abuse was paramount.

Personal possession of obscene material in the home may not be prohibited by law. In 1969, the Court ruled that *if the First Amendment means anything, it means that a State has no business telling a man, sitting in his own house, what books he may read or what films he may watch.* However, it is constitutionally permissible for the government to prevent the mailing or sale of obscene items, though they may be viewed only in private. In 2002 the Court further upheld these rights by invalidating the Child

Pornography Prevention Act of 1996, holding that, because the act *prohibited child pornography that does not depict an actual child* it was overly broad and unconstitutional under the First Amendment and that:

> *First Amendment freedoms are most in danger when the government seeks to control thought or to justify its laws for that impermissible end. The right to think is the beginning of freedom, and speech must be protected from the government because speech is the beginning of thought.*

In 2008, the Court upheld the Protect Act of 2003, ruling that prohibiting offers to provide and requests to obtain child pornography did not violate the First Amendment, even if a person charged under the Act did not possess child pornography.

CHAPTER TEN: Incarcerated Books[11]

In some U. S. states, there are laws prohibiting convicted criminals from publishing books for profit. These laws were a response to offers made an individual to write memoirs about the murders he committed. The Supreme Court struck down a law of this type in New York as a violation of the First Amendment in 1991. That statute did not prohibit publication of a memoir by a convicted criminal. Instead, it provided that all profits from the book were to be put in escrow for a time. The interest from the escrow account was used to fund the New York State Crime Victims Board – an organization that pays the medical and related bills of victims of crime. Similar laws in other states remain unchallenged.

The US English term *incarcerated Books* refers to *a Son of Sam* law which is a term for any law designed to keep criminals from profiting from the publicity of their crimes, often by selling their stories to publishers. While the term is most often used in the United

States, it is also sometimes applied to laws passed with similar provisions in other nations.[12]

Abuse of the First Amendment

Speech Freedom

CHAPTER ELEVEN: Libel and Slander[13]

In 1964 a prominent justice wrote the landmark decision that requires the demonstration of *actual malice* in libel suits against public figures.

American tort liability for defamatory speech or publications traces its origins to English common law. For the first two hundred years of American jurisprudence, the basic substance of defamation law continued to resemble that existing in England at the time of the Revolution. In 1898 an American legal textbook on defamation provides definitions of libel and slander are nearly identical to those given by other justices. An action of slander required the following:

Actionable words, such as those imputing the injured party: is guilty of some offense, suffers from a contagious disease or psychological disorder, is unfit for public office because of moral failings or an inability to discharge his or her duties, or lacks integrity in profession, trade or business;

That the charge must be false;

That the charge must be articulated to a third person, verbally or in writing;

That the words are not subject to legal protection, such as those uttered in Congress; and

That the charge must be motivated by malice.

An action of libel required the same five general points as slander, except that it specifically involved the publication of defamatory statements. For certain criminal charges of libel, such as seditious libel, the truth or false of the statements was immaterial, as such laws were intended to maintain public support of the government and true statements could damage this support even more than false ones. Instead, libel placed specific emphasis on the result of the publication. Libelous publications tended to *degrade and injure another person* or *bring him into contempt, hatred or ridicule.*

Concerns that defamation under common law might be incompatible with the new republican form of government caused early American courts to struggle between the argument that the punishment of *dangerous or offensive writings . . . was necessary for the preservation of peace and good order, of government and religion, the only solid foundations of civil liberty* and the argument that the need for a free press guaranteed by the Constitution outweighed the fear of what might be written. Consequently, very few changes were made in the first two centuries after the ratification of the First Amendment.

The Supreme Court's ruling in 1964 fundamentally changed American defamation law. The case redefined the type of *malice* needed to sustain a libel case. Common law malice consisted of *ill-wil* or *wickedness*. Now, a public officials seeking to sustain a civil action against a person who commits the wrong doing needs to prove by *clear and convincing evidence* that there was actual malice (the person committing the act is called a tortfeasor). The case involved an advertisement published in a New York newspaper indicating that officials in Alabama had acted violently in suppressing the protests of African-Americans during the civil rights movement.

The Alabama Police Commissioner sued the newpaper for libel, stating that the advertisement damaged his reputation. The Supreme Court unanimously reversed the large judgment against the newpaper. A justice suggested that public officials may sue for libel only if the publisher published the statements in question with *actual malice*, the *knowledge that it was false or with reckless disregard of whether it was false or not*. In sum, the court held that *the First Amendment protects the publication of all statements, even false ones, about the conduct of public officials except when statements are made with actual malice, that is with knowledge that they are false or in reckless disregard of their truth or the fact of being untrue.*

While actual malice standard applies to public officials and public figures, in 1988, the Court found that, with regard to private individuals, the First Amendment does *not necessarily force any change in at least some features of the common-law landscape.* In 1985, the Court ruled that *actual malice* need not be shown in cases involving private individuals, holding that *in light of the reduced constitutional value of speech involving no matters of public concern . . . the state interest adequately supports awards of presumed and punitive damages—even absent a showing of 'actual malice.* In 1974, the Court ruled that a private individual had to prove actual malice only to be awarded punitive damages, but not to seek actual damages. In a magazine case of 1988, the Court extended the *actual malice* standard to intentional infliction of emotional distress in a ruling which protected parody, in this case a fake advertisement in the magazine suggesting that an evangelist's first sexual experience had been with his mother in an outhouse. Since evangelist was a public figure, the Court ruled that *importance of the free flow of ideas and opinions on matters of public interest and concern* was the paramount concern, and reversed the judgement that evangelist had won against the magazine for emotional distress.

In 1990, the Court ruled that the First Amendment offers no wholesale exception to defamation law for statements labeled *opinion*, but instead that a statement must be provably false before it can be the subject of a libel suit. Nonetheless, it has been argued that other cases effectively provide for an opinion privilege. In consequence a significant number of states have enacted state opinion privilege laws.

Speech Freedom

CHAPTER TWELVE: States and Speech[14]

State constitutions provide free speech protections similar to those of the U.S. Constitution. In a few states, such as California, a state constitution has been interpreted as providing more comprehensive protections than the First Amendment. The Supreme Court has permitted states to extend such enhanced protections, most notably in a Californian case in 1980. In that case, the Court unanimously ruled that while the First Amendment may allow private property owners to prohibit trespass by political speakers and petition-gatherers, California was permitted to restrict property owners whose property is equivalent to a traditional public forum like shopping malls and grocery stores from enforcing their private property rights to exclude such individuals. However, the Court did maintain that shopping centers could impose *reasonable restrictions on expressive activity*. Subsequently, New Jersey, Colorado, Massachusetts and Puerto Rico courts have adopted the doctrine and California's courts have repeatedly reaffirmed it.

Abuse of the First Amendment

Speech Freedom

CHAPTER THIRTEEN: The Press[15]

Free speech and free press clauses have been interpreted as providing the same protection to speakers as to writers, except for wireless broadcasting which has been given less constitutional protection. The Free Press Clause protects the right of individuals to express themselves through publication and dissemination of information, ideas and opinions without interference, constraint or prosecution by the government. This right was described in 1972 as *a fundamental personal right* that is not confined to newspapers and periodicals. In 1938, one justice defined *press* as *every sort of publication which affords a vehicle of information and opinion*. This right has been extended to media including newspapers, books, plays, movies, and video games. While it is an open question whether people who blog or use social media are journalists entitled to protection by media shield laws, they are protected equally by the Free Speech Clause and the Free Press Clause, because both clauses do not distinguish between media businesses and nonprofessional speakers. This is further shown by the Supreme Court consistently refusing to recognize the First Amendment as providing greater protection to the institutional media than to other speakers. For example, in a case involving campaign finance laws the Court rejected the *suggestion that communication by corporate members of the institutional press is entitled to greater constitutional protection than the same communication by* non-institutional-press businesses.

A landmark decision for press freedom came in 1931, in which the Supreme Court rejected pre-publication censorship. In this case, the Minnesota legislature passed a statute allowing courts to shut down *malicious, scandalous and defamatory newspapers*, allowing a defense of truth only in cases where the truth had been told *with good motives and for justifiable ends*. In a 5–4 decision, the Court applied the Free Press Clause to the states, rejecting the statute as unconstitutional. One justice quoted Madison in the majority decision, writing: *The impairment of the fundamental security of life and property by criminal alliances and official neglect emphasizes the primary need of a vigilant and courageous press.*

The leak of the Pentagon Papers led to a 1971 landmark press freedom decision. However, the justice also noted an exception, allowing prior restraint in cases such as *publication of sailing dates of transports or the number or location of troops.* This exception was a key point in another landmark case four decades later in 1971, in which the administration of the President sought to ban the publication of Pentagon Papers as classified government documents about the Vietnam War secretly copied by the analyst. The Court found, in a 6–3 decision, that the Administration had not met the heavy burden of proof required for prior restraint. One justice, drawing on the work of the prior justice wrote a concurrent opinion, that stated: *only governmental allegation and proof that publication must inevitably, directly, and immediately cause the occurrence of an evil kindred to imperiling the safety of a transport already at sea can support even the issuance of an interim restraining order.*

Two justices went still further, writing that prior restraints were never justified.

The courts have rarely treated content-based regulation of journalism with any sympathy. In 1974, the Court unanimously struck down a state law requiring newspapers criticizing political candidates to publish their responses. The state claimed that the law had been passed to ensure responsibility. The Supreme Court found that freedom, but not responsibility, is mandated by the First Amendment and so it ruled that the government may not force newspapers to publish that which they do not desire to publish.

Content-based regulation of television and radio, however, have been sustained by the Supreme Court in various cases. Since there is a limited number of frequencies for non-cable television and radio stations, the government licenses them to various companies. However, the Supreme Court has ruled that the problem of scarcity does not allow the raising of a First

Amendment issue. The government may restrain broadcasters, but only on a content-neutral basis. In 1978, the Supreme Court upheld the Federal Communications Commission's authority to restrict the use of *indecent* material in broadcasting.

State governments retain the right to tax newspapers, just as they may tax other commercial products. Generally, however, taxes that focus exclusively on newspapers have been found unconstitutional. In 1936, the Court invalidated a state tax on newspaper advertising revenues, holding that the role of the press in creating *informed public opinion* was vital. Similarly, some taxes that give preferential treatment to the press have been struck down. In 1987, for example, the Court invalidated an Arkansas law exempting *religious, professional, trade and sports journals* from taxation since the law amounted to the regulation of newspaper content. In 1991, the Supreme Court found that states may treat different types of the media differently, such as by taxing cable television, but not newspapers. The Court found that *differential taxation of speakers, even members of the press, does not implicate the First Amendment unless the tax is directed at, or presents the danger of suppressing, particular ideas.*

In 1972, the Court ruled that the First Amendment did not give a journalist the right to refuse a subpoena from a grand jury. The issue decided in the case was whether a journalist could refuse to *appear and testify before state and Federal grand juries* basing the refusal on the belief that such appearance and testimony *abridges the freedom of speech and press guaranteed by the First Amendment.* The 5–4 decision was that such a protection was not provided by the First Amendment. However, a concurring opinion by one justice stated that a claim for press privilege *should be judged on its facts by the striking of a proper balance between freedom of the press and the obligation of all citizens to give relevant testimony with respect to criminal conduct. The balance of these vital constitutional and societal interests on a case-by-case basis accords with the tried and traditional way of adjudicating such questions,* has been frequently cited by lower courts since the decision.

Speech Freedom

CHAPTER FOURTEEN: Summary

In this text on the First Amendment to the United States Constitution, the emphasis is primarily on Freedom of Speech and Freedom of the Press. The definition of *freedom* in America has been evolving since the birth of the nation. The words *clear and present danger* are important to note when considering the First Amendment. They occur many times in the text especially with reference to *Freedom of speech*. It also must be noted however that *balancing test*, supplanted the *clear and present danger* test.

The topics covered in this book include:

Chapter One: **Change** The author talked about the social issues in *freedom from want* that is juxtaposed with *free enterprise*. He talked about freedom coming to be defined more and more by the boundary of race and slavery which has done a lot to shape the language and idea of freedom. He said that terms like *wage slavery* and *sex slavery* exist because *slavery* came to embody the notion of a lack of freedom.

Chapter Two: **Article** Deals with the thought that the makers of the Constitution were concerned about the meaning of words. The article word 'the' is closely looked at since it is used frequently as in *the freedom of speech,*

Chapter Three: **Government Criticism** In World War I the mood of the country gave rise to the Court paying close attention to the *Alien and Sedition Laws* and whether they played a *clear and present danger* to the country. It also talked about *Passing Protection Along* and the *Free Speech Clause* which led to the Smith Act, making it illegal to advocate overthrowing or destroying any government in the United States by force and violence. In each case the Courts asks whether the gravity of the 'evil' justifies invasion of free speech as necessary to avoid the danger. Clear and present danger did not intimate that before the Government should act that it must wait until the violent overthrow is about to be executed.

The Court discussed the words *Fuck the Draft* and one justice wrote in the majority opinion that a jacket fell in the category of protected political speech despite the use of an expletive saying *one man's vulgarity is another man's lyric*.

Chapter Four: **Politicians** The Court talked about literature and pamplets. In 1960, the Court struck down a Los Angeles city ordinance that made it a crime to distribute anonymous pamphlets. They also discussed flag desecration. The divisive issue of flag desecration was termed a form of protest which first came before the Supreme Court in 1969. They discussed Money and Finance. In 1976, the Supreme Court reviewed the Federal Election Campaign Act of 1971 and related laws, which restricted the monetary contributions that may be made to political campaigns and expenditure by candidates.

Chapter Five: **Forcing** The Court determined that the United States Government could not compel students to recite the Pledge of Aliegiance.

Chapter Six: **Money in Talking** Commercial speech is done on behalf of a company or individual for the purpose of making a profit. Unlike political speech, the Supreme Court does not afford commercial speech full protection under the First Amendment.

Chapter Seven: **Education** In 1969, the Supreme Court extended free speech rights to students in school. The case involved several students who were punished for wearing black armbands to protest the Vietnam War.

Chapter Eight: **The Web** The internet is a descitful and insidious medium, however the Court has applied its tests of Freedom of Speech to it.

Chapter Nine: **naughty stuff**, One Supreme Court Justice wrote that while he could not precisely define pornography, he *knew it when he saw it*. The federal government and the states have long been permitted to limit obscenity or pornography.

Chapter Ten: **Incarcerated Books** In some U. S. States, there are laws prohibiting convicted criminals from publishing books for profit.

Chapter Eleven: **Libel and Slander** In 1964 a prominent justice wrote the landmark decision that requires the demonstration of *actual malice* in libel suits against public figures.

Chapter Twelve: **States and Speech** State constitutions provide free speech protections similar to those of the U.S. Constitution.

Chapter Thirteen: **The Press** Free speech and free press clauses have been interpreted as providing the same protection to speakers as to writers, except for wireless broadcasting which has been given less constitutional protection.

In all cases the determining factors deal basically with two tests;

   1) *balancing test* which is based on the
   2) *clear and present danger test*

Even in the cases of *Libel and Slander* the same tests above apply to where *actual malice* has to be proven. The first test needs to be taken with the second or there is much room for argument. In all the various topical cases the key word is *speech* taken in the context of the two tests. Basically if the topic is agreed to be *speech* does the case present a *balanced, clear and present danger?*

Although keep in mind that the The Court held that *a fundamental principle of the First Amendment is that all persons have access to places where they can speak and listen, and then, after reflection, speak and listen once more.*

Speech Freedom

ABOUT THE ATHOR

Jess Browning is former Director of Global Trade,
Transportation and Logistics Studies at the University of Washington in Seattle. He has and MPA Degree from the University of Southern California and a Ph.D. from the University of Washington in Seattle.

At the local level he served on the Freight Mobility Roundtable; at the national level he served on the Transportation Research Board's International Trade and Transportation Committee; and at the International level he served as a U.S. Delegate to APEC's Transportation Working Group.

In retirement, he helped form a Consortium of eight international universities to do joint research an education in the fields of business, advanced technologies, logistics and marine affairs.

Jess is a former entrepreneur having engaged in manufacturing and global trade. He holds eight patents in environmental and process control equipment.

He believes that economic development takes place at many scales that includes: *from what takes place on the plant floor to what takes place in various regions of the world.* He finds no difficulty in moving from one to the other in order to promote economic development.

Jess is and author of thirty four books and has edited five more with more to follow. He has given many talks, lectures and keynote addresses at home and abroad. He is married and lives with his wife near Seattle. They have 4 daughters, 6 grandsons, 4 granddaughters and 4 great granddaughters with 1 great grandson and another known to be on the way.

INDEX

arrested, 36, 47

Arthur, 11

assembly, 36, 60

Association, 21

attack, 24, 32

attacks, 24

author, 5, 17, 27, 63, 106

authorities, 69

avoid, 37, 98

B

b, 68

battled, 21

behalf, 53, 100

believed, 28, 36

believes, 106

Bible, 11

birth, 21, 22, 97

black, 36, 59, 100

Black, 9, 10

boundary, 22, 97

Britain, 10

British, 67

Browning, 3, 5, 10, 105, 131

Brownings, 9

browsing, 64

building, 34, 68

burned, 47

burning, 39, 47

business, 54, 69, 77, 106

businesses, 90

C

Caleb, 10

California, 10, 85, 105

campaign, 43, 44, 90

campaigns, 44

candidate, 45

Captain, 9, 10

Carolina, 63

Caroline, 10

Carrie, 17

cast, 47

center, 24

century, 31, 48, 67

challenge, 45

court, 32, 33, 37, 39, 44, 54, 67, 68, 80

Court, 22, 27, 31, 32, 33, 34, 35, 36, 37, 38, 39, 43, 44, 45, 46, 48, 51, 53, 54, 55, 56, 59, 60, 63, 67, 68, 69, 70, 73, 79, 80, 82, 85, 90, 91, 92, 93, 94, 99, 100

courts, 37, 79, 85, 90, 92, 94, 98

create, 33

created, 22

creating, 93

crime, 43, 47, 73, 99

crimes, 73

criminal, 36, 38, 73, 78, 91, 94

criminals, 73

critical, 17, 31

cycle, 46

D

damage, 78

danger, 33, 34, 37, 39, 70, 94, 97, 98, 99

dangerous, 31, 79

daughters, 17, 106

decades, 91

deceitful, 63

decided, 69, 94

decision, 37, 39, 43, 47, 48, 49, 60, 68, 77, 90, 91, 94

decisions, 6, 22, 39

deed, 6

defense, 33, 90

definitive, 27

Degree, 105

Delegate, 105

delivered, 34

Democratic, 60

desire, 92

destroying, 37, 98

destruction, 39

determined, 51

development, 106

Director, 105

L

labor, 22, 35

laid, 37

Lancelot, 9, 11

landmark, 77, 90, 91

landscape, 81

language, 22, 24, 97

large, 22, 80

late, 27

law, 19, 27, 28, 31, 32, 37, 38, 39, 44, 47, 48, 56, 63, 69, 73, 77, 79, 81, 82, 92, 93, 131

lawful, 55, 63

laws, 35, 44, 70, 73, 74, 78, 82, 89

lead, 27

leaders, 37

leading, 31

least, 45, 81

leaving, 69

lectures, 106

led, 91

legal, 51, 77, 78

legislation, 28

less, 89

level, 22, 105

liability, 77

life, 90

light, 59, 81

likely, 39

limit, 67, 100

limits, 28, 44, 46

list, 53

listen, 63, 102

literature, 43

little, 67

local, 69, 105

location, 91

logistics, 106

Logistics, 9, 105

Love, 10

lower, 37, 94

M

major, 21

make, 45

man, 39, 69

Man, 10

manufacturing, 106

marine, 106

Marshall, 28

Massachusetts, 85

master, 23

material, 6, 67, 68, 69, 93

matter, 54

means, 5, 36, 69

measures, 28

mechanical, 5

medical, 73

member, 53

members, 68, 90, 94

mentioned, 5, 27

Merchant, 10

military, 13, 32, 48

Miller, 69

Minnesota, 90

Mobility, 105

money, 44, 45, 64

months, 45

Mordred, 11

movement, 24, 80

moving, 106

MPA, 105

murder, 47

N

Nanci, 17

narrow, 28

narrowing, 27

nation, 21, 31

national, 23, 33, 38, 44, 69, 105

National, 47

nations, 74

natural, 34

nature, 17, 33

nearly, 77

necessarily, 81

need, 60, 79, 81, 91

News, 21

Nomads, 10

North, 63

novel, 67

number, 21, 35, 82, 91, 92

Speech Freedom

REFERENCES

---

[1] http://gould.usc.edu/about/news/?id=1202 by Lori Craig, Friday, Nov 16, 2007.

[2] First Amendment to the United States Constitution, https://en.wikipedia.org/w/index.php?title=First_Amendment_to_the_United_States_Constitution&oldid=805640275 (last visited Dec. 11, 2017).

[3] First Amendment https://en.wikipedia.org/w/index.php?title=First_Amendment_to_the_United_States_Constitution&oldid=805640275 (last visited Dec. 11, 2017).

[4] Ibid.

[5] Ibid.

[6] . Ibid.

[7] . Ibid.

[8] . Ibid.

[9] Browning, Jess, "The Deceitful and Insidious Web" 2017

[10] First Amendment https://en.wikipedia.org/w/index.php?title=First_Amendment_to_the_United_States_Constitution&oldid=805640275 (last visited Dec. 11, 2017).

[11] Ibid.

[12] Son of Sam law, https://en.wikipedia.org/w/index.php?title=Son_of_Sam_law&oldid=797821094 (last visited Dec. 12, 2017).

[13] First Amendment https://en.wikipedia.org/w/index.php?title=First_Amendment_to_the_United_States_Constitution&oldid=805640275 (last visited Dec. 11, 2017).

[14] Ibid.

[15] Ibid.